A GENTLE REMINDER

BIANCA SPARACINO

AMARYLLIS

AMARYLLIS

An imprint of Manjul Publishing House Pvt. Ltd.
• C-16, Sector 3, Noida, Uttar Pradesh 201301, India
Website: www.manjulindia.com
Registered Office:
• 2nd Floor, Usha Preet Complex, 42, Malviya Nagar, Bhopal 462 003 - India
Distribution Centres
Ahmedabad, Bengaluru, Chennai, Hyderabad,
Kochi, Kolkata, Mumbai, Noida, Pune

A Gentle Reminder by Bianca Sparacino

This edition first published in India in 2024
Fourth impression 2025

ISBN 978-93-5543-848-5

Printed and bound in India by Thomson Press (India) Ltd.

for the deep feelers

The right person will know how to hold your love. The right person will choose you just as deeply as you choose them. You will not have to quiet the way you care, you will never feel like you are too much. You will not have to beg for the love you deserve. One day, you will be met where you are. One day, you will be someone's favorite thing, and you will not be confused — you will not feel like you are fighting for someone who isn't fighting for you. One day, you will understand that it never mattered how tightly you held on to the wrong people, how intensely you tried, because the right people were always going to find you. The right people were always going to stay.

Remember — even the strongest souls get exhausted. The strongest human beings, the ones who laugh the loudest and hope the hardest, the ones who are always there for others — those souls often need people there for them. So, please — check on your kind friends. Check on the people in your life who are tender, the ones who are always open to give so much of who they are for those who need it. Check on the people in your life who love with every ounce of their being, who feel deeply and care deeply, and try to fix and mend and make sure that those around them are okay. Please, just check on the people in your life who are brave, who are soft for this world. Check on the people in your life who protect others at all costs — because those souls need protecting, too. Those souls need to be reminded that they deserve the love they keep giving to everyone else.

You have to let go. You have to let go because when you hold on, when you keep something alive inside of you, you are allowing for your past to take up the space in your heart and in your mind that is meant for your future. You have to let go because at the end of the day, if you are going to find the human being who is going to bring you the deepest kind of joy, if you are going to find the person who is going to help you experience the kind of love you have always deserved — you have to make sure that you are ready for it. You have to make sure that you will be open to it, and you cannot make a home within your heart for the person who will someday care for you in the softest of ways if someone else's memory is still living there. You have to let go. You have to accept that sometimes beautiful things end, that sometimes people leave, that sometimes two human beings don't beat the odds, and you have to find closure in that. You have to heal. You have to move forward, you have to believe in the version of you that is laughing in bed on a Sunday morning with the person they love twenty years from now, because you deserve that future. It is waiting for you. Choose it.

It is okay to take your time. We live in a generation that romanticizes moving forward as quickly as possible when it comes to careers and our futures and our success within them. But there is no point in rushing quickly towards a life that will not inspire you or fulfill you. It is okay to slow down. It is okay to take the time you need. You are in no rush to figure out your own soul. It's never too late to start over, it's never too late to change your mind, it's never too late to redirect yourself, to replace the dreams you thought you wanted for the ones that genuinely excite and challenge you.

So keep going — because the world needs your uniqueness. It needs your talent, your art, your mind. The world needs you to take up space within that, so you can change it with the vision that you have. You are so deeply capable of doing something beautiful with your life. Don't let roadblocks, or self-doubt, or the way your journey is unfolding convince you otherwise. Leap towards all that scares and ignites you. Just try for something while you're here.

If it is for you, trust
that it will find you.

Maybe right now, your journey isn't about love.

Maybe right now, your journey is about being alone. Maybe this is the season you are being challenged — to learn how to wake up in the middle of the bed, to finally find hope in the vacancy, hope in the quiet, hope in the way you stretch into your life and give yourself permission to take up space within it. Maybe right now, you are being shown — that you can take care of yourself, that you can depend on the person you have become, that you can be your own home no matter what comes your way.

Maybe right now, your journey is about redemption. Maybe this is the season you are being challenged to make amends with your heart, to stand up for the vast ways in which it loves, and cares, and believes in the goodness of vulnerability, and expression, and being the person who softens even when the world is not gentle. Maybe right now you are getting a second chance — to trust in it, and to forgive yourself for giving it away to those who could not value it; but most importantly, maybe right now you are being called to protect it, to find your way back into your tenderness, to find your way back into your soul.

No, maybe right now your journey isn't about love. Maybe right now your journey is about hope. Maybe this is the season you are being challenged to remind yourself of the beauty life has to offer you. Maybe right now, you are being given the space to discover the kinds of places that leave your bones dripping with feeling, the kinds of songs that are yours and yours alone, the kinds of people who love you in a way that does not seek to change you. Maybe right now, you are being given a chance to reclaim your joy, to make it the most natural extension of who you are, to let it spill out of your words, and your laughter, and your tears — to let it be something you believe you are worthy of, to let it be something you believe you deserve.

See, maybe right now your journey isn't about love. Maybe right now your journey is about you. Maybe this is the season you are being challenged to be your own savior, to be your own safe place. Maybe right now you are being reminded — that the people who walked away were only ever leading you back to yourself, were only ever leading you here. And here, you are okay on your own. Here, you are rebuilding. Here, you are adapting, and mending, and reclaiming all of the pieces you let them walk away with. Here, you are being kinder to your soul, you are giving yourself the same kind of love you have always given to others. Here, you are not rushing your heart, you are not depending on another human being to fix it. Instead, here, you are doing that on your own. Here, you are healing.

When you are ready to put your heart into this world again, do not look for the same kind of love you have experienced; resist the urge to compare the human beings that come into your life to the ones that have left. Because the truth is — two loves will never be the same. Love is like a fingerprint, curated between two individual souls, and within that it is always its own rare and beautiful thing, an extension of who you both were within those moments in time. In moving on, in dealing with the breaking and the rebuilding of your heart, you grow. You become a different person, and in turn the love you need, the love that will nourish you and inspire you and meet you where you are now — that grows as well. That changes.

When you are ready to put your heart into the world again, do not look for the kind of love you recognize, for the kind of love that mirrors something that did not beat the odds. Instead, search for the kind of love you need — as you are, in this season of your life. Do not compare it or doubt it when it arrives, because it will be different. It will always be different. It will hold you differently, and it will say your name differently, and it will laugh differently, and hope differently, and you will make different memories within it; you will feel it in your bones in a way that you won't be able to express, in a way that will feel new and somewhat scary, but right. Do not seek familiarity, do not keep searching for your past in your future. Trust what comes.

No one will ever fully be able to understand the internal battles you had to endure just to heal, just to grow, just to make it here today. Be proud of the way you fought to save yourself. Be proud of the way you survived.

If something ignites you — chase it. Chase it, because you don't want to look back in two years, or five years, or twenty years and wonder what would have been. Chase it, because you don't want to think back to all of the potential, and all of the beauty, you missed out on because you were afraid, or because you let an idea of yourself that was untrue rob you of your joy or your capacity to move confidently in the direction of the things that inspired you. Chase it — because you can, because you deserve to experience what is profound and remarkable in this world, because you are worthy of the things that make your chest tighten with happiness and wonder. Chase it, because you never know what is waiting for you on the other side of your comfort. You never know what is waiting for you on the other side of your hope.

I hope you have the courage to keep loving deeply in a world that sometimes fails to do so. In a generation that orders up attention like they order up a meal, in a generation that has started to love with one foot out the door, I hope you have the courage to believe that genuine connection still exists. And I hope you have the courage to stand up for that, to open yourself to it when you start to feel it bloom within the heart of you. I hope you have the courage to appreciate it for all that it is, to not approach it wearing a mask, to not try to desensitize yourself to it or play it cool. Please, I hope you have the courage to crash your heart into the people life gifts you. I hope you have the courage to believe that goodness still exists, that there are those who have the capacity to love the way you do, that there are those who will see you and grow you and teach you more about the world. I hope you have the courage to fight for connection. I hope you have the courage to go deeper. To never exist on the surface of your life, even if it's easier or more convenient. At the end of the day you should leave this world with a heart that is worn-out and soft all over. A heart that is bruised from loving, and feeling, and caring in the best way possible. At the end of the day, you should be proud of your inability to be anything but open to the world. You should be proud of who you are.

I hope you have the courage to do the hard work. I hope you have the courage to sit down with your demons, to befriend them; to look them in the face and to not feel fear. I hope you have the courage to stop picking or numbing or avoiding the wounds within, and I hope you choose to heal them instead. I hope you have the courage to understand yourself, fundamentally — to open up the deepest, darkest parts of your mind, to unhinge your rib cage revealing the gritty parts of your soul, the parts no one else claps for, and I hope you have the courage to clean them out. To forgive yourself for what you had to do to kill your sadness. To forgive yourself for the ways in which you didn't fight for the person you were becoming. I hope you have the courage to nurture your pain, to not disregard it or sweep it under the rug of distraction or convenience. I hope you have the courage to heal yourself, even when it hurts.

I hope you have the courage to know when to end things. And I hope you have the courage to see endings as beautiful, transformative stepping stones. I hope you have the courage to let love and opportunity move through you like rain. To not grip, or seek to change it, to not ask people or circumstances to be more than they can be for you. I hope you have the courage to see endings as the cornerstones of the chapters that changed you without needing them to be a part of the rest of your story.

And when that is done, I hope you have the courage to give yourself closure. To be your own home. To be your own safe place. I hope you have the courage to not let the losses destroy you, to not let them burrow into the heart of who you are and convince you that you failed, or that you are unworthy of the happiness you are standing up for in your life. I hope you have the courage to see the way in which you loved and tried and fought for something as a testament to just how deeply your capacity to feel is, just how beautiful moments can be when you appreciate them for what they were instead of nullifying them or letting them harden you to the world. Please, I hope you have the courage to move forward. I hope you have the courage to walk away with grace.

I hope you have the courage to do things differently, to be the kind of person who takes the risk, to be the kind of person who leads with their heart and shows up in their life with a ruthless dedication to learning and growing and enjoying the hell out of their moments here. I hope you have the courage to never let comfort or apprehension convince you that you are better off staying still. I hope you have the courage to trust the part of yourself that knows there's more out there for you, the part of yourself that is easy to quiet when you're trying to live by the rules and the expectations of a world that has bred so much dissatisfaction and sadness. I hope you have the courage to trust the part of yourself that seeks freedom from those trends, from those boundaries, and I hope you have the courage to go after whatever it is that genuinely makes you want to get up in the morning. I hope you have the courage to find the things in life that ignite you and deepen your understanding of the world and those within it. I hope you have the courage to fight for a future that inspires you, even if it doesn't look the way you thought it would. I hope you have the courage to change. I hope you have the courage to trust in the person you're becoming.

Listen to the part of yourself
that knows there's more
out there for you.

The kindest people are not born that way, they are made. They are the souls that have experienced so much at the hands of life, they are the ones who have dug themselves out of the dark, who have fought to turn every loss into a lesson. The kindest people do not just exist — they choose to soften where circumstance has tried to harden them, they choose to believe in goodness, because they have seen firsthand why compassion is so necessary. They have seen firsthand why tenderness is so important in this world.

You deserve to be loved the way you love others. You deserve to feel seen. You deserve to sleep beside someone who does not try to quiet your heartbeat, or your passion, or the way you show up in this world. You deserve to be with the kind of person who loves all of your twists and does not try to untie them. You deserve to love someone who does not judge you for the ways in which you had to kill your sadness, someone who does not hold your past against you. You deserve to be chosen and to never be loved in halves. You deserve someone who is sure of you; you deserve someone who stays.

However, you also deserve to be this person for yourself. For your capacity to be alone, your capacity to be your own home, your own foundation, is going to directly reflect the way you love these human beings when they come into your life. When you know yourself, when you stand up for your heart, you do not bankrupt who you are just to keep half-loves in your life. Love becomes less about filling a void, love becomes less about possession, less about dependence, and it transforms into something that can be fully and deeply appreciated and felt, because you are not afraid that its loss will destroy you. You are not afraid of being without it, because you know that you will always have yourself.

The bravest thing
you will ever do
is learn how to love
the things that made you.

If you are trying to forget someone who was once a beautiful part of your life, the answer is — you don't. You don't try to sanitize your experience, you don't try to cut the pain from the bone. You don't downplay it. You don't try to sweep it under the rug or hide it away. Letting go of someone you thought would be in your life forever is difficult; sometimes circumstance gets in the way. Sometimes, no matter how much love is there, you have to lay it down. You have to walk away. You have to accept that sometimes you get too big for it, or you want different things, or you cannot pour yourself out for it any longer. And that is okay.

But if you managed to find someone who cared for you, who saw you, who heard all of the horrible and haunted things you did in your life and still loved you harder, still thought it all shone like gold — that is special. You shouldn't forget that. You should be thankful for it.

Be thankful that you got to feel that way about someone.

Be thankful for all of the mornings, and all of the nights, you got to wrap your limbs within theirs.

Be thankful for the way they cracked your heart open.

Be thankful for the way they challenged you and calmed you and made you believe in the person you were becoming.

Be thankful for the fact that they saw you in ways you didn't see yourself.

Be thankful for the fact that you risked for love, that you unhinged your rib cage and opened yourself up in a world that sometimes favors playing it cool over leaping towards connection.

Be thankful that you found this person, in a world of billions, and for a moment in time, even if it was fleeting, you got to dive into the soul of them.

Just be thankful and walk away with grace. Walk away with gratitude. Walk away knowing that you felt something, that you experienced something a lot of people haven't, and in that way — you were changed. Love is not meant to be possessed. It is meant to be felt. Be proud of yourself for feeling so deeply, appreciate it for what it was, and let that love go off into the world and change others the way it changed you.

Move on — not for anyone else, not to prove to anyone that you can, but rather, do it for yourself. Do it for your future. Let go of what is heavy within you. Move forward with the lessons, carry them inside of yourself. Move on, not because you have something to prove to the outside world, but because you have something to prove to your heart, you have something to prove to your soul. You are worth saving. Save yourself.

I think it's beautiful — the way you show up in this world, unguarded and willing to try again, despite all of the ways it has tried to defeat you. I think it's beautiful, the way you tuck courage into yourself each morning, the way you refuse to be anything but hopeful in this world, despite the inner battles you fight, despite the struggles you have experienced for so long. I think it's beautiful — the way you twist your losses into lessons, the way you fight even when you feel weak. You are not weak. There is a resounding level of courage to be found in being the person who continues to heal, even when it hurts. There is a resounding level of bravery to be found in being the person who believes in the light, even when they cannot see it.

You will not find a love that is perfect, but you will find a love that is real.

You will not find a love that is perfect, but you will find a love that sees you. The kind that brings down your walls, that asks you to share the parts of your soul you have tucked away and kept hidden from the world. You will not find a love that is perfect, but you will find a love that shows you that it is okay to be the kind of person who balances both hope and hurt within them, that it is okay to be the kind of person who has not always known how to quiet the beating of their heart within their chests. And this love, it will hold you there. It will not vilify you for the ways you have to heal your sadness, for the ways you show up in this world. This love, it will not flinch at the sight of your darkened past — it will hold you there. Not just when you are a gleaming example of beauty or perfection, but when you are baring your teeth. When you are unraveled before it. It will not run from you when you take off your mask.

You will not find a love that is perfect, but you will find a love that connects. This love, it will not shy away from the depth of you. It will dive. It will sit you down and ask you about your childhood home. It will ask you what it felt like to lose your mother, what it felt like to always be the person who never quite fit in. This love, it will know you. And on some levels, it will feel like it always has — that you have been carrying around a longing for it that on some level your soul was always waiting to reconnect with its heart, was always waiting to come back home to the parts of itself you eventually found in another human being.

You will not find a love that is perfect, but you will find a love that reminds you that goodness exists. This love, it will inject honey into the soul of you, it will feel like warmth has cracked within your bones. And you will see how it learns you, and fights for you, and stays to weather the storms by your side. You will be reminded that there is connection in a world that often chooses distance over depth. You will be reminded that there is hope to be found pouring from the fingertips of another human being, tucked between the layers of the things you have yet to discover about them. No, you will not find a love that is perfect, but you will find a love that is light, that isn't heavy to carry, that does not weigh down the core of you. You will finally understand that love was always meant to be soft. That it was always meant to be tender.

No, you will not find a love that is perfect — but you will find a love that reminds you just how worthy you always were. This love, it will show you that you were never asking for too much, that the way you sent your heart to war for other human beings was not foolish, that the way you were incapable of loving in halves was not wrong. This love, it will show you that it was always okay to be the kind of person who loved in a way that was full, and nourished, and hopeful all over. That it was always okay to be the kind of person who could never shy away from their heart. This love, it will make up for all of the times you were asked to slaughter your instincts, for all of the times you tried to break yourself down just to comfort or impress someone who was not meant for you. This love, it will show you that you were always worthy of it, that you always deserved to be seen and understood, that you always deserved to be held and cared for the way you held and cared for all that came before it. This love will teach you — that you were never too much. You were always enough. You were always enough.

Make your mind
a beautiful place to be.

One day, when you least expect it, you are going to crash into someone who is going to be so soft and gentle with your heart, and you are going to be so glad you kept it open. You are going to be so glad that you continued to fight for it — that you chose to believe it deserved more.

You were never
asking for too much.

You were simply just asking
the wrong person.

Forgive yourself for changing. Forgive yourself for being a different person than you were a year ago or three months ago or even a week ago. Forgive yourself for wanting different things, and for maybe stepping away from the goals or the dreams or the people you fought to manifest in your life.

Sometimes, it's extremely difficult to see change, to see that difference within your own soul and your own desires as a good thing. But it is a good thing; it's the best thing, because it means that you're learning. It means you're asking questions. It means you're not settling in your life, it means that you're not just taking a back seat to the way you crash your heart into this world, it means that you are asking more from yourself, it means that you are genuinely trying your best to figure out what deserves to stay in your life, instead of just keeping things within it because they are there.

Forgive yourself for changing. And more importantly — be the person who changes. Because when you are the person who changes, it means you are the person who is growing. Instead of vilifying yourself for that, instead of feeling like you are falling away from yourself, use this transformation as a reminder that you are actually falling into yourself. That you are actually chasing the kind of life that is going to be the best reflection of the season you are in. And do not fear that change, do not get so comfortable in your life that you aren't moving at all, that you aren't taking chances or asking questions about how the things within it are truly, deeply making you feel. Wish for change. It doesn't mean that you're lost. It means that you're finding yourself.

Forgive yourself for giving your heart to those who could not love it or value it. Forgive yourself for falling for the wrong people. Because they weren't the wrong people — you were meant to meet them, you were meant to fall for them, you were meant to experience them and learn from the lesson. You do not have to regret the way you put your heart into the world. You do not have to vilify yourself for feeling, and for caring, and for hoping that something beautiful you felt with another human being would turn into something real and tangible and pointed.

When you're mending your heart, it can be difficult to see that. When you're mending your heart, it can be difficult to come to terms with the fact that, at times, you may not have fought for what it deserved. Maybe you stayed longer than you knew you should. Maybe you wish you would have seen the signs earlier, that you could have walked away before the damage was done, before the lesson was learned in a really hard and haunted way.

At the end of the day, when you care deeply, when you're empathetic, when you believe in love and the beauty of another human being so deeply — sometimes, you can convince yourself to fight wars for someone who isn't fighting for you, sometimes you can convince yourself to keep trying, or to not give up, but that isn't something to be ashamed of. You tried for something, you risked, and even though it did not work out, you in return learned how to set boundaries, how to go forward with your heart and protect it — not in a way that is guarded and hardened to the world, but rather in a way that is informed, that helps for it to be preserved and nurtured, that doesn't let it settle for things that aren't for it. Now you know what you do not want. Now you know what you do not want to feel. Now you know the kinds of things you crave, the respect you deserve, and you won't settle for the opposite any longer. Forgive yourself for how you got to that understanding.

Forgive yourself for taking your love back. Forgive yourself for outgrowing certain people in your life. Forgive yourself for all of those moments you had to protect your energy, for all of those moments you had to make the hard decision to choose yourself, because by staying, and trying to fight harder, and give more, and be more, and fix and fix and save and save, you were only ever depleting yourself to the point of exhaustion. Forgive yourself for all of the times you tore up pieces of your own heart in order to mend another human being, hoping that it would heal them and nourish them and make them better or happier. Forgive yourself for wanting to save the people you loved.

Understand that sometimes, in order to do that, you have to walk away. Because you cannot fix the people you love. You cannot heal them. They have to do that on their own. And if someone isn't showing up for that healing, if they are content with having you hold them together, then that will only ever ruin you. Walking away to refuel yourself, giving your heart a break, allowing for it to be yours and yours only, allowing for the love you so compassionately poured into another human being to be poured back into yourself — that is something you need to forgive yourself for. Because not only were you choosing to nurture yourself, but you were also helping this person in a way you may not fully comprehend.

Sometimes the most formative way to love another human being is to love them from a distance, is to lay down your hope and your fight, is to know when to wave the white flag and challenge them to show up for themselves. You were not put into this world to fix people who do not want to be fixed. It is okay to walk away from relationships that require you to do so. Forgive yourself for that.

Forgive yourself for the way you treated yourself in the past. For the way you talked to your body. For the way you vilified the way your mind worked when you were dealing with anxiety, or overthinking, or depression, or anything that was haunting it. Forgive yourself for the way you settled for less than what you wanted, or desired, or knew you needed, because you didn't think you deserved it; because you convinced yourself, somewhere along the lines, that you were not worthy of beauty in life, that you were not worthy of happiness or goodness or having the things you wanted come to fruition. Forgive yourself for the way you held yourself back because you didn't believe in your own potential, because you didn't believe in your capacity to take up space. Forgive yourself for all of the things you didn't say, or didn't wear, or didn't do because you were afraid of how it would make you look, because you were afraid of what others might think of you. Forgive yourself for the way you didn't show up for yourself. For the ways in which you held yourself back, for the ways in which you didn't see just how worthy you were. For the ways in which you made yourself smaller.

Forgive yourself for the things you had to do in order to survive. For the ways in which you had to fight through the pain of navigating all that was heavy and messy and confusing along your journey.

Do not vilify yourself for the ways in which you had to comb through your sadness, for the ways in which you had to learn how to quiet your mind and protect yourself from all that was trying to bury you. Forgive yourself for what you had to do in order to heal. Forgive yourself for the ways in which you fought. Forgive yourself for the ways in which you saved yourself. Forgive yourself for doing whatever you had to do to ensure that you made it to see another day.

It is okay if you hid from the world. It is okay if you weren't as productive as you needed to be. It is okay if you let relationships slip, or if you let yourself slip. It is okay if you felt depressed, or sad, or anxious as you met your healing. It is okay. However you fought your battles, whatever got you here today is valid. You had to do what you had to do. Congratulate yourself on having the courage to do it, even if it was not graceful, even if it could have been executed in a kinder way or a more tender way, even if you see now that you could have done things differently. It is okay.

Be gentle with yourself. You were learning.

You still are.

Maybe the universe fights for certain souls to find one another. And maybe the universe places people in your life just to take them away, just to teach you the things that beauty cannot. Maybe the universe fights for the heartbreaks, for the missed opportunities, for the bad timing. Maybe the universe knows in an offhand way, that those moments will show you your strength in ways the hope cannot. Maybe it is within the losses that you truly find gratitude for all that has stayed. Maybe it is through caring for those who make us feel like we are hard to love that we are taught how to embrace those who see us, those who truly protect our souls. And maybe, just maybe, it is through the darkened journey that we are taught how to appreciate the warmth, how to chase the light.

We want to protect the people we fall in love with. We want to nurture them and hold them where they are their most tender; we want to make sure that they know we are not revolted by their broken pieces, that we do not recoil at their damage. We want to hold it all, we want to whisper into the cracks, "It's okay to be who you are with me." We do this because we see so much of ourselves within those we give our hearts to. We notice the ways the fragments of their personalities and their experiences and the way the characteristics life has given them glint in the light and catch our attention, most likely because we see within them a familiarity. We may not have been broken in the same way, weathered in the same way, but we still feel a sense of belonging to them, a sense of being understood. In a way, it is through loving those broken pieces within another human being that we are kinder to the pieces that ache in the same ways within ourselves. We may not always call it by its name, but in the quiet, almost eerie, understanding that hangs in the air when you are in the presence of someone who sees you in ways the others don't, something deep inside of you is affirmed. Maybe, just maybe, it is okay to believe that you can be loved there, too. Maybe, just maybe, it isn't such an unthinkable thing to have faith in.

Give yourself permission to let go of what weighs heavily on your soul. You carry it all so well, but that does not mean that it is yours to hold.

Listen — if you are in love with someone who cannot love you back at the moment, please understand that this is not a reflection of your goodness, this is not a reflection of your worth. Sometimes life weathers people in different ways. We are all on this Earth just trying to figure ourselves out, just trying to mend the breaks in our souls, just trying to deal with what is heavy within us. Sometimes we're ready and another person is not. Sometimes we try and another person does not. Sometimes we pour ourselves into another human being and they cannot contain all that we are. Sometimes we fight and another person surrenders. Sometimes we choose to make things work, and another person decides that they cannot choose that same reality. And that is okay. I need you to understand that is okay.

Because at the end of the day, if someone does not meet you where you are, you cannot keep asking them to do so. If someone cannot reciprocate your love, if someone cannot give you what you truly deserve, you have to understand that aching for them to do so before they are ready is a form of self-destruction. Your heart is a vast and tender thing; you cannot keep trying to shrink it into what someone else needs. You cannot keep pouring your love into a vessel that cannot contain it. You cannot keep pouring your love into a soul that has not opened their eyes to all that they are receiving. You cannot keep pouring your love into a heart that is closed off to it. It will only leave you empty. You have to walk away. You have to let this person grow on their own terms, because you can't love someone into their potential. You can't love someone into being ready. They have to do that on their own.

And I know how hard it is to walk away from someone you deeply care for. I know how hard it is to lay all of that love down, to close your heart off to all that it sees in another human being. But in walking away you will learn how to pour all of the love that you were giving to the wrong person back into yourself. And you will learn how to pour it into all that you desire in life, you will learn how to pour it into your growth, into your art, into your hope. You will learn how to stand up for your feeling, how to stand up for its value. And when you teach yourself that you deserve to be loved, without having to beg for that love, without having to chase that love down, you open yourself to the kind of beauty that chooses you just as freely as you choose it. You open yourself to the kind of people who see you and immediately know that you are a rare and beautiful thing. You open yourself to new beginnings, to a future that unfolds in ways that don't hurt or break you down, but rather build you up and show you just how worthy you are of having your heart held.

Being loved openly and clearly builds the most uniquely beautiful connections. At the end of the day, nothing is more attractive than someone who stands firmly in front of you and chooses you. At the end of the day, nothing is more comforting than the kind of love that grows from certainty and conviction — no games, just presence.

Maybe you will never get back to the person you used to be.

But maybe that is okay. Maybe that is something to celebrate, something to embrace, because who you were is a version of yourself that exists in the past. A version of yourself that didn't go through the heartbreak or the hardship; a version of yourself that did not have to navigate all of the ways in which life was trying to weather it. Who you were is a version of yourself that didn't have to fight their way out of the dark, that didn't have to deal with the things that caused change to crack within the soul of you — and those things transform a human being.

Maybe you will never be reintroduced to that version of yourself. Maybe you will never get back to who you were. Maybe that version of yourself has evolved, has grown, into who you were meant to be at this moment in time. Maybe you have to lay down that expectation, maybe you have to release that comparison, and instead, maybe you have to trust in the lessons and the ways in which the world has asked you to stretch towards your becoming. Maybe you have to stop looking backwards.

Molting is the process by which a snake routinely casts off its skin to facilitate new growth, and sometimes life forces you to do the same. Sometimes, life challenges you to shed relationships, and ideals, and the old versions of yourself that no longer serve you. So when you feel like you are not the same person, when you feel like you have unraveled, like you have evolved into someone you do not recognize, maybe that is something to honor. You have transitioned, you have transformed, and life will ask you to do so time and time again as you journey through it. Do not fear your evolution. Claim it.

The truth is, when you settle for an almost, you settle for almosts in every single aspect of a relationship. Almost happy. Almost valued. Almost chosen. Yes, the connection holds weight, there is depth there, but it will always exist on the surface of what your soul craves. When you settle for an almost, you're left waiting to receive the kind of love you have been giving someone all along, you're holding out for something real, and pointed, and full, to grow from so much uncertainty. But you deserve more than that. You deserve certainty. You deserve to be someone's favorite thing. You deserve effort, you deserve for the beauty you see within another human being to come to fruition, to be something substantial, to be something you can grow within. You deserve to feel like someone is excited to be with you, like someone is excited to commit to you, like someone is inspired to dive into something concrete and foundational with you. You deserve someone who is on the same page. Someone who wants the same things, someone who wants to meet all of your hope with action. You deserve someone who isn't afraid of being responsible for your heart. You deserve someone who embraces it.

When you are not feeling good enough, remember that even at your best, you will not be good enough for someone who does not have the capacity, or the will, to love you. And while there is a very human part in each and every soul that leaps towards needing to prove ourselves, to care more, to try harder just to demonstrate our worth, at the end of the day, if someone does not see the value that is pinned and blooming within you, it doesn't matter what you do. It doesn't matter how hard you fight for someone who isn't fighting for you. It doesn't matter how hard you show up for someone who isn't showing up for you. It doesn't matter — because those human beings don't actually see you. If they did, they would respect you, they would value you because you deserve to be valued, they would cherish the rare and magnetic hope you have to offer because it deserves to be cherished. Don't ever forget that the right people will choose you, they will see you, they will dive into the depth of you, and you will never have to force those connections. You will always be good enough for them. Anything else is not for you.

When you are not feeling good enough, remember that sometimes the root of feeling not good enough comes from holding yourself to someone else's ideal rather than your own. Remember that you are the only person who gets to decide if you are good enough. You are the only person qualified enough to determine your value. Please, do not put your happiness, or your self-love, or your belief, into the hands of other people or their validation or understanding of you. Do not make it contingent on their acceptance of you, or their willingness to love you or care for you or choose you. All you have to focus on is building the kind of life that is yours, and yours alone. All you have to do is focus on building yourself into the kind of person you are proud of. You are in charge of your worth. Nothing can externally dictate that, nothing has that power, unless you give that power of yours away. Don't give that power away. Make yourself happy on your own terms.

When you are not feeling good enough, just try your best to remind yourself how far you have come. Start paying attention to what you are, rather than what you aren't. Start paying attention to the things you have, rather than the things you don't. Remind yourself that you are someone's favorite human being. Remind yourself that you have overcome the most hurtful and haunted aspects of life. Remind yourself that while sometimes your journey may feel like it is being weathered by circumstance or difficulty, while there are going to be days where the dark and the doubt crack within the soul of you — you have defeated those days before. And as simple as that may sound, it is important to remind yourself of the strength you have fostered, it is important to remind yourself that the things you thought would once destroy or bury you never had the capacity to do so. There is worth in that strength. There is worth in that growth. It will always exist within you, even when you cannot feel it.

Please, if you have forgotten, if you do not feel good enough right now, remember that you are worthy, and deserving, of everything you want in life. You deserve to fall in love with someone who cares for you in the softest way, someone who drives you and believes in you and is always in your corner, not just when it is easy, but when it is hard. You deserve to be that person for yourself as well. You deserve to be surrounded by people who grow your mind, people who make you better because they push you to be better. You deserve the kind of confidence that makes you believe that anything is possible, the kind that empowers your voice and your ideas and your capacity to seek out the things that you desire. You deserve moments of pure and intense happiness, the kind that make you feel your heart beating against your chest, the kind that dizzy you and make you realize that everything will be okay, that you will be okay. You deserve to be chosen. You deserve to be loved the way you love others. At the end of the day, you deserve to be inspired by your life.

To be who you are,
after all you have been through
at the hands of this world,
is beautiful.

We live as if we are promised the experiences and the potential we are chasing, we live as if we have control over what happens to us. But we don't, and that is liberating, because it is pressing — there is urgency within the lesson. It wakes you up.

Remember — you are not promised tomorrow. So how are you going to ensure that you crash your heart into your life? How are you going to ensure that you leave this world, whenever it happens for you, with a soul that is tender and full and weathered in the best way? With a soul that was never asked to make itself smaller, with a soul that was never waiting for the day it was skinnier, or prettier, or cooler, or more successful, in order to take advantage of the time it was given?

We cannot wait to be the people we have always dreamed of being. We cannot wait for life to perfect itself. There is no right time, there is no perfect circumstance. We have to leap, even when our legs are shaking. We have to show up for ourselves — not in 3 months, or 5 years, or 10 years, but now. In this moment. Because every single day is a blessing. Every single day is a gift. Do not lose sight of that.

The truth is, you cannot skip certain chapters in your life. Sometimes, you have to experience the wrong love in order to learn how to fight for your heart, in order to learn how to recognize the right love when it comes your way. Sometimes, you have to be alone, you have to heal in the quiet, so that you do not let your past wounds stop you from receiving all that you deserve in this life. Sometimes, you have to choose the wrong path, you have to make the mistake, in order to truly connect with the fact that even the missteps, that even the rejections, were really just redirections. Sometimes, you have to lose all that you hoped for yourself, all that thought you wanted, in order to unearth all you truly need, in order to make room within your life for the right things to unfold. Remember — everything you once considered a failure was really just an opportunity to flourish. Everything you once considered an error was really just an opportunity to expand into the kind of life that you were always meant to be living, into the kind of love, and career, and happiness that were always meant to be yours.

It is okay to be affected by something you thought you had healed from. Healing is not linear. Be gentle with yourself.

Listen — I know it's hard. I know it's hard to live without someone who was once a hopeful part of your life. I know it's hard to wish that they were beside you through the difficult times, I know it's hard to see something beautiful and not have your heart ache with the urge to experience it with them. I know what it is like to live in the aftermath of another human being.

I know it is hard; I know it hurts. But you cannot focus on the people who walked away, you cannot keep all of that hope alive inside of you. At the end of the day, if someone wants to be in your life, they will be. Truly — they are capable, they will make the effort, they will show up. If they do not — let that be your closure.

However, you do not have to hate them. You do not have to remember their contribution to your life as anything but beautiful. Do not ruin them in your mind, do not grip until you feel resentment. Instead, love them without attachment. Love the lessons they taught you. Wish them well every single time you think about them. Miss them, but do not ache for them to come back. If the people in your life left because they were not ready to value you, or love you, or be there for you, do not wish for them back, do not ask for them to be more than they can be at the moment. Wish for them to figure themselves out. Wish for them to grow. They are on their own journey — a journey you are not a part of. And that is okay. You have to learn that that is okay.

So instead of focusing on the people who left, focus on the people in your life who have chosen to be there. Focus on the ones who stayed, on the ones who appreciate you and respect you. Focus on the people who match the love you give them, focus on the people who empower you and grow you and make your life beautiful. You are surrounded by human beings who will not shy away from the love you give. You are surrounded by human beings who know that they want you in their life, people who show you that every single day. Do not take them for granted. Do not lose touch of what you have, chasing what you no longer do.

Trust me when I say — you will miss out on beautiful things if you continue to stay rooted in all of the ways you were wronged, if you continue to let your past pull you from experiencing what the present has to offer you. Do not close yourself off to your potential. Instead, open yourself to the world, and allow for it to fill that space with the kinds of people, the kinds of moments, and the kinds of experiences that exhilarate you, that compel you — that make you love yourself, and your life, and what you have to offer, more and more each day.

No person is sent to you
by accident.

Sometimes, love doesn't win. Sometimes beautiful things end because you outgrow another human being, sometimes love becomes too heavy to hold — the potential and the lessons and the evolution have reached a threshold, there is nowhere else to place your hope. However, that is not something you should deem a failure or something that should break your heart. That is something to celebrate. You managed to care for someone in the deepest way, and you grew one another into human beings who are going to go off into this world and change other people with that love. You did all that you could for one another, and instead of forcing something that wasn't working or fulfilling you anymore, you chose to walk away. You chose to release your grip, to believe that there were other things in store for your hearts. There is bravery in that.

When you feel like giving up:

Remember that your left lung is smaller than your right lung, simply to make room for the heart you hold within your chest. At your most primal level your heart was favored; it took precedence. It will never be incapable of growing, it will never cease to hold the whole damn world within it, so do not try to stop it.

Remember that you use 200 million cells to take one step forward. Do not vilify yourself for the journey you have walked thus far, for it has taken effort and every single aspect of your body has conspired to help you get to where you are.

Remember that you shed your tired skin every twenty-seven days. You were not made to hold your past within you, you were not made to carry it all on your back. You physically let go of every bad thing that has ever touched you, of every pair of foreign hands that unbuttoned your shirt but never your demons; you let go of every regret, of every insecurity. You are always gifted a clean slate.

Remember that your tongue is the strongest muscle in your body. You were made to speak — so speak loudly and honestly about how you feel. Speak about what hurts you, about what has broken you. Speak about your story, share it with the world.

Remember that the carbon in your body is the same carbon that courses through this Earth, that makes up mountains. Let this remind you that you can stand alone, you can stand tall, for just like Everest, just like Fuji, you are a force to be reckoned with.

Remember that the bones within your body are as strong as granite. You are never broken, you are never weak. When you feel like you couldn't possibly bear the weight of heartbreak, of growth, remember that your foundations are stronger than concrete. You were made to endure, you were made to withstand.

Repeat after me: You were made to survive. Every single part of you, every single perceived flaw and every single aspect of who you are, was made with the intention of defying the odds. You were bred from tough, celestial pieces of this world, and therefore it will never be able to defeat you.

You can do hard things. You can do hard things, and not because you will be unaffected and bulletproof within your growth, not because you are immune to breaking down, not because you will find it easy to navigate all that is healing within you. No, your journey is never going to be faultless, is never going to be devoid of pain, but you can do hard things, because you show up to do them, even if it is imperfectly. Even when it hurts. Even if you break down. Even if you feel tender. No matter how weathered you feel, no matter how lost you feel, you can wake up in the morning, you can do whatever you have to do in order to tuck the light between your bones, you can do whatever you have to do in order to remind yourself that goodness exists, that you are capable of finding it, that things are always going to be okay.

You can do hard things. You are strong enough to live without them. You are strong enough to become the person you have always wanted to be. You are strong enough to let go, to walk away, to ask for what you need, to stand up for yourself and your heart and the life you truly want to live. You can do hard things, no matter how difficult they are. Whatever you do, please, just believe in that. Keep going. Nothing is going to defeat you. Nothing has the capacity to destroy you, unless you give it permission to. So keep going. You're going to look back on these moments in your future, and you are going to be so glad that you trusted in your healing. You are going to be so glad that you chose to believe that there was more for you.

The love you deserve will choose you just as confidently as you choose it. The love you deserve will fight for what you have when difficulty hangs heavy in the air, it will insist that you are stronger together, that you are capable of beating the odds, that you are filled with the potential to turn your losses into lessons — into seeds that will make it stronger. The love you deserve will be your voice of reason; it will calm the soft creature you are when doubt sinks into your skin, it will build your restless heart a safe place within itself.

The love you deserve will love you unapologetically, and that beauty, that softness, will inspire you to believe in the human being you are becoming. The love you deserve will see gardens within you where you see cemeteries. It will reflect its vision into your eyes, it will show you the way the world sees you. The love you deserve will support you, it will ruthlessly believe in your mind, it will celebrate your depth. The love you deserve will be proud of you — not just when you are a shining example of yourself, but also when you are not. The love you deserve will love you, even when you do not deserve it.

The love you deserve will clap for the parts of yourself you always used to hide, it will cherish the twists within your soul that others always wanted to untie. The love you deserve will peek into the most profound parts of who you are, and it will cradle you there. It will not cower, it will not run away. The love you deserve will be your best when you are not your best. It will show up for you in the dark.

But most importantly, the love you deserve will teach you how to trust in the timing of your life. How to trust in the fact that it was always going to find you. The love you deserve will teach you how courageous it is to simply have faith in the heart of another, how difficult and messy and beautiful vulnerability can be after years of hurt. The love you deserve will teach you that you were never too much for those you always tried to give your soul to. You were always enough. You were just giving your heart to the wrong people. You were always worthy.

Maybe the hardest seasons of life teach you a different version of happiness. Maybe in those seasons, the things you live for, the things you value most, seem so small in comparison to what you were filling your soul with in the past, seem so quiet in contrast. Maybe it is within those moments that your eyes are opened, that you learn how to find joy, and peace, and safety in that which you didn't even notice before.

Maybe in the seasons of life where your heart aches, or loss has built a home within you, happiness changes. Maybe it becomes your morning cup of coffee — sitting and drinking it as the sun rises and the world wakes up around you. Maybe happiness becomes the way the light plays with the trees in your favorite park; maybe it is the way the sky looks at your favorite time of night, the way the moon fills the air with an energy you can feel in your bones when you really sit with yourself and let your solitude wash over you. Maybe in the messiest moments of life, happiness is your mother's voice. Maybe it is the beauty you feel when you see your friends' faces, when you hug them for twenty minutes straight, when you sit with them in silence and feel so understood, and so seen, in all that you are.

Maybe in the most complicated moments — happiness simplifies in a deeply profound way. Maybe it exists in the songs you listen to and the way your pen scratches across your journal in the morning. Maybe it exists in the quiet, in the moments where you fully connect with yourself and you love yourself and you are kind to yourself in all that is gritty and all that is hard and all that is unanswered in your life.

Maybe the hardest seasons of life teach you that happiness is small. That it exists in the stillness, that it echoes through you in the most nameless moments. And maybe the hardest seasons of life teach you that those moments aren't small at all. That those fleeting experiences, that those simple encounters, have always been saving you, have always been the things that mattered.

It is okay to outgrow those who don't know how to love you.

Please, just trust the timing of your life. You don't have to have it all figured out by a certain age; you don't have to chase a version of success that does not inspire you. You just have to learn about yourself. You have to keep doing the work — not just physically, but emotionally. You have to learn about who you are on a foundational level, you have to understand what you deeply value, what ignites your soul, what makes you want to get up in the morning, and you have to choose that every single day. You have to stand up for it. You have to leap towards that hope, even when it's scary, even when you're the only one dreaming in that direction.

Because there's no point in moving quickly towards a life you don't want. There's no point in doing everything right if you are just going to end up unhappy. No—you are not failing at life. You are not falling behind because you are moving at a different pace than those around you. You are not odd, or delusional, if your dreams do not look like the ones society told you to have when you were younger. You are making your life your own. You are growing into your future. Never be ashamed of that.

I hope you learn how to let go.

I hope you learn how to let go of everyone's opinion of your life. I hope you start to see, from a place that lives deep within you, that there is no universally correct way to live a life that is solely your own. Every human being has different goals, has different concepts of what happiness looks like, has a different concept of what it truly means to be alive. And because of that, people will judge you — the world will try to change you, but you must continue to move in your own direction, you must continue to go at your own pace, because if you allow for that to alter your path you're going to end up living someone else's life. I hope you learn how to make your life your own. I hope you learn how to make your time here something you are proud of.

I hope you learn how to let go of the comparison you hold so closely to your chest. I hope you strive to dismantle the distractions, I hope you strive to see beyond what is manicured and what is filtered in this life. You are a real human being who is living and breathing in this world, who is healing through and moving through seasons of beauty and seasons of change and seasons of evolution each and every single day. Your experience in this world will never be perfect, will never be faultless — but it will be real. It will be honest. I hope you learn how to embrace that.

I hope you learn how to let go of your tendency to favor distance over depth. I hope you learn how to open to this world, how to let love pour into your life. We often protect ourselves from seeming too eager or too interested; we hold our feelings back because we don't want to seem overly emotional or tender. We silence our instincts, we bankrupt our souls, and at the end of the day we feel alone. I hope you learn how to let go of your fear, I hope you learn how to remind yourself that there is nothing wrong with vulnerability, with being human, with unhinging your rib cage and sharing your heart with this world. There is beauty to be found in being the person who cares. So care.

I hope you learn how to let go of a love that won't love you back. I hope you learn how to let go of the stories you tell yourself, of the ways in which you have let all that has hurt you, all that has bruised your soul, convince you that you needed to settle for less than what your heart desired. I hope you learn how to let go of the parts of yourself that make you feel like you are not worthy of the kind of love that teaches you and hopes for you. But above all else, I hope you learn how to let go of the idea that you cannot be this person for yourself. You are your own safe place. Make your alone a beautiful place to be.

Most of all, I hope you learn how to let go of the idea that it's too late. It is never too late to change your life. It is never too late to become the person you have always hoped you could be, or to love the way you have always wanted to love. We often forget that we are not bound by our past. We don't have to be who we were a year ago, we don't have to make the same mistakes we did when we were younger; we can want different things, we can grow. We have to believe that we are never too old, never too jaded, and never too broken to take our first steps towards change. We wake up every single day with the ability to start fresh — it is never too late to take advantage of that. It is never too late.

In a society that has taught us to favor being cool over being connected, promise yourself that you will always choose to be the person who cares. To be the person who does not desensitize themself, to be the person who slams their heart into the people who excite it without hesitation, without worrying if it is too much or too intense or too loud. Trust me when I say that you will never scare off the souls that will fully understand you, and nurture you, and celebrate you, by being open to this world, by being honest, by being the kind of person who loves deeply. Do not water yourself down, do not silence the parts of yourself that leap towards the beauty you see in another human being. Be all that you are. Be all that you are.

Sometimes you break your own heart. Sometimes you stay longer than you know you should, because you hold so much hope within you. Learning how to lay down that hope is one of the hardest parts of the healing process, but it is where you begin again. Trust yourself enough to let go, even when it hurts.

If you were capable of feeling so much towards those who may not have always been gentle with your heart, imagine how beautiful love will be when it is right — imagine how beautiful love will be when it stays.

One of the hardest lessons you will ever have to learn in life is that you do not need closure to heal and move on from something that had to end, from the kind of love you had to set down.

One of the hardest lessons you will ever have to learn in life is that closure doesn't actually serve you. Closure is a way that we hold on when we don't want to let go. Closure is a way we look to cut the pain from the bone, a way we try to bandage our hearts, but when we do get it, if we ever do, it never makes things easier. It doesn't patch our souls back together immediately. We still have to heal from the loss. We still have to hold all of the memory, and all of the potential, and all of the work inside of ourselves. We still have to learn how to carry all of that weight.

And the truth is — closure doesn't change that. Closure might add reasoning to the healing, but it will not heal you. Often we think it will — that we will hear the words, that someone will explain that they fell out of love, that someone will admit to not wanting to nurture our hearts anymore, that someone will admit the horrible, hurtful things we imagine in our heads, and we will feel better. But it won't make anything better, it won't dissolve the hurt. The ache will just hurt differently.

And so, when we grip to closure, when we wait for it, when we make our healing contingent on what someone else is providing for us, we put our healing into their hands. In that way, we never let go until they allow us to. We never let go until they give us permission to let go.

But letting go doesn't happen when we have reasoning or permission to let go. Letting go happens when we come to terms with the fact that someone wasn't our person, that a relationship wasn't our forever, that we have to move forward and go into the world and find those who want to love us and care for us, because we deserve it. And isn't that something we can give to ourselves?

At the end of the day, if someone has decided that they cannot love you anymore, you have to let them go. And this is a difficult emotion to hold within a human heart; this is a difficult lesson to learn. It is okay to find this heavy, it is okay to struggle with moving on from the unknowns. But we have to forgive people for not being able to love us, or leave us, the way we deserved to be loved and left. We have to forgive human beings for not knowing what they wanted, for not being at a point in their own healing or emotion to be gentle with our hearts. We have to forgive the people we have lost for leaving the way they left.

Because when we forgive the situation, we say:

"While this may hurt, and while I may never understand why I had to break this way, this circumstance cannot, and will not, keep me here in this hurt. It will not keep me here in this feeling, in this resentment, in this pain. I choose to let this pain go. I cannot keep this ache alive inside of me. I have to feel it, acknowledge it, and let it go. I have to give myself my own understanding, I have to move forward, I have to give myself permission to allow the chapter to go unmended, to allow the loose ends to stay loose, to not grip at needing a perfect conclusion, but rather, to rewrite my healing and my story in a way that allows for me to go out into the world and find what I truly deserve. To find what was actually for me."

We have to gift ourselves the closure we so deeply desire. We have to take responsibility for our feelings and understand that we cannot wait for someone to give us our healing. We have to heal ourselves. We have to move forward — no matter how badly we think we were treated, no matter how difficult and how dark it feels, we have to move forward and we have to remind ourselves that we have the capacity to heal ourselves. We have to stop giving away our power. We hold our own power, we hold our own hearts, and we hold our own healing. We have to let the people who do not want to be in our lives go, we have to stand within the voids and the space they left, and we have to rebuild there.

That is where the heart mends. That is where the scars heal. And that is something you give yourself. No one else is going to do it for you. No one else is capable.

Please, if you are waiting for closure to move on, I hope you give yourself permission to let go. I hope you give yourself permission to let something end in the middle of a chapter. I hope you give yourself permission to connect with the fact that no closure is closure. That a half-ending is still an ending.

That someone not being able to choose you anymore just means that they were not meant to hold your heart. You can add meaning to that, you can dress it up, or dress it down, you can seek to understand why, but that does not change the fact that the universe did not fight for your souls to beat the odds, it does not change the fact that this person cannot love you.

And you deserve to be loved the way you love others. You deserve someone who celebrates your heart. You deserve someone who wants to hold you for twenty minutes straight on a bad day and make you breakfast in bed and laugh at all of your horrible jokes. You deserve someone who respects you enough to be honest with you. You deserve someone who communicates, who nurtures your soul, who does not run from the love you have to give. You deserve this. You deserve to find it in this world because it exists. That kind of genuine love exists, and you can start working towards opening your heart to it today. Not tomorrow, and not when you get an explanation, but now.

You are brave enough to heal here. You are courageous enough to save yourself. And while this is hard, and while it may not make sense, it is within these moments that you truly can connect with just how strong you are. With just how deeply you can stand up for yourself, and your heart, and your capacity to be your own home, your capacity to heal in even the most unfair or dark circumstances. Choose your own healing. Take it back. Know that it is a gift you give yourself.

One day it hits you — that you spent so much of your life closed to the world. That you spent so much of your life trying to protect yourself from the love you craved, that you gave so much of your energy to a version of existence that was cut off from believing in the beauty, in the good, as a form of survival.

One day it hits you — that if there is any magic in this world, it exists in being seen by other human beings, in connecting. One day it hits you — that if there is any magic in this world, it exists in being unguarded and vulnerable; it exists in allowing for yourself to surrender to your hope. It exists in not being afraid of what life is trying to teach you, in not allowing yourself to run from what is asking to be felt within your soul.

One day you just open. The cost of staying fortified and hidden away becomes too high. One day, you lay down your arms. You let love rush in. You let it wash over you. You crack your shell, you expose your heart to this world, and you trust that you are worthy of being seen there. You trust that you are worthy of being known there.

When you're the person who is always there for others — you feel a lot. You have depths within you, an ocean for a heart, and you sometimes fall for people who are too afraid to swim. You give and you give and you give. You never know how to stop yourself from pouring into those you love.

And so, there are moments where a tender ache sometimes forms within your unhinged chest. There are moments where you are left wondering if someone will ever give you the love you so freely give to others, moments where you wonder if there will ever come a time when someone asks how you are doing, how you are coping, how you are healing.

See, sometimes the person who is always there for everyone else needs someone there for them. Sometimes, the person who smiles the biggest holds the biggest hurt. Sometimes the person who encourages everyone around them needs to be told that they are appreciated, that they matter; sometimes they need to be encouraged, sometimes they need to be held — no matter how strong they seem, no matter how brightly they shine.

So, if you're the person who is always there for others, know that your heart is rare. Know that you hold within you an ability to calm storms in people. Know that you give people hope, that you inspire them by acknowledging the pieces of them most ignore, that you make people feel wanted, that you make people feel like they have purpose. That you make people feel seen.

However, also remind yourself that you are not invincible. Your heart needs rest. You need rest. Remind yourself that you do not need to carry the weight of the world on your shoulders, that you may not be able to save everyone, that you may not be able to heal every hurt. Remind yourself that you deserve to take all of the energy you put out into the world and invest it back into yourself from time to time. That you are worthy of the love you keep giving to everyone else. Remind yourself that you don't always have to be strong, that you don't always have to be the fixer. Remind yourself that you can be human, that you can ask for help, that you don't always have to be the one to save yourself.

It is quite simple — nothing that is meant for you will ever get away. Love deeply and without the need to possess or own; let beautiful connections pass through you without attachment, slam your heart into the people and the places and the things that ignite something deep inside of your soul, and I promise, I promise — the right things will stay. You will never lose what is for you. Please don't ever forget that.

Learn how to heal yourself
from one person
without needing another.

When you have been hurt before at the hands of another, it can be difficult to convince yourself to risk your heart, it can be difficult to convince yourself that there are those in this world who will keep it safe, who will protect it. When you have been hurt before, despite wanting to experience love again, you can let the what-ifs hold you back.

What if you fall for someone and they leave? What if you place your heart in the hands of someone else and they do not want to hold it? What if they do not love you back? But what if they do?

What if you take the chance, what if you risk your heart, what if you crash it into someone who genuinely inspires you, and they choose you? What if they love you the way you always desired to be loved? What if they make you breakfast in bed on Sundays, and hug your broken pieces back together, and bring you soup when you're sick, and fill your life with the sunniest, most tender kind of happiness? What if they grow you, and encourage you, and teach you that love was always meant to be soft? That it was always meant to feel the way it feels when you are with them? What if they make you understand why it never worked out with anyone who came before them? What if they stay?

And what if they do leave? What if there does come a time where they cannot be what you need? What if you outgrow one another, what if you evolve into two people who cannot beat the odds? What if love changes, but what if there is still gratitude there? Gratitude for the way in which they stretched your heart into what it ended up becoming, gratitude for how they helped for you to find clarity in what you desire and what you strive to find in the next person life gifts you? Does that make it any less important, any less rich? Does that make it any less worthy of being felt, of having the kind of depth and connection that might not last forever, but that breeds the kind of lessons and knowledge and hope that will?

Do not be afraid to follow your heart.

Do not be afraid to try for something.

Instead of vilifying yourself for staying longer than you should have, for giving your heart to those who could not hold it, instead of getting upset that you settled — celebrate the fact that you've opened your eyes to all that wasn't growing you, celebrate the fact that you had the courage and the strength to walk away. Celebrate the fact that you are aware now.

It is beautiful to be the kind of person who searches for love in a culture that is obsessed with lust. Because lust can be so boring, it can be so cliche. Often it is empty, it is transparent, it holds no weight. We are a society that has been taught to chase the shiniest things, to fill our lives with beauty for beauty's sake, to focus more on attaining and possessing and devouring rather than sitting with and diving into the things that actually mean something to us. We mistake what our eyes want for what our hearts want, and that is one of the most dangerous things we could do to ourselves. It kills our humanity, because it kills our presence. We taste, but we do not savor. We touch, but we do not feel. We talk, but we do not connect.

It is okay to have a soul that still believes in depth, in the kind of connection that exists beyond the surface. Do not try to bankrupt your need for more, do not try to quiet the way your heart slams into your chest. Do not envy those who leap towards lust or longing like it is going to change their lives. Those people, I have found, are often looking to either escape themselves or distract themselves, and it bankrupts them. They are empty in certain ways, always after the next beautiful thing and the next after that. They devour, and devour, and devour, but they will never be full. They are malnourished where it counts; they will never be satisfied. Because the real nourishment, the real feast, exists not in someone's lips or the curve of their spine. It exists in the most honest aspects of who they are. It exists in their nostalgia and in their hopes and in the way certain songs make them want to cry.

You want genuine beauty? Real beauty? The kind of connection that isn't short-lived, but rather feels like it has existed for hundreds of years? The kind of connection that feels all-consuming and feverish and grounding at the same time?

Connect.

Sit with someone and ask them about all of the horrible things they have done in their life, and listen to the way their voice cracks. Sit with someone and let them tell you about what it felt like to lose their dad, what it felt like to break the heart of someone they once loved. Sit with someone and look them in the eyes, hold their hand, listen to the way they talk about the things they are passionate about, how their smile curves towards their ears. Sit with someone and let them touch you. Not physically, but mentally. Sit with someone and let them have you, not tangibly, but on a soul level. Only then will you understand why lust is so vacant in comparison, why it is so dull.

And I know. I know it can be hard to believe in genuine connection when the world sometimes feels like a hard and haunted place, when people dig into the soul of you just to warm themselves by the fire of your hope. But I promise, it exists.

Because I know what it is like to hold a human being at their most tender. I know what it is like to feel a person's heart, beating so in unison with your own that it feels like it is a living, breathing part of your own body. I know what it is like to have someone's energy flowing through you like rain, I know what it is like to walk away with pieces of their memory tattooed to your skin. To have fragments of another soul tangled in your hair, pressed into the backs of your knees, strung like Christmas lights along your spine, bookmarked and dog-eared to the deepest corners of your mind. I know what it is like to be seen. To be truly seen, in all that shines for the world and all that is grotesque and dark and hidden from the masses. I know what it is like to open, to flay all of the vulnerability from one's bones, to bloom towards being known.

I know what it is like.

It exists. Never stop searching for it.

When you feel like things will never get better — think about all of the things in life that have tried to defeat you. Think about all of the moments that hung heavy in the air, the moments that had you convinced that you would never find light within the darkness of it all. Think about all of the times you thought to yourself that your heart would never mend, that all of the ways in which you risked for it and weathered it were finally taking their toll, that there was no way in which you could come back from the loss or the break. Think about the moments, think about how convinced you were that you would never find the strength to move forward.

And then connect with the fact that you are still here. You are still alive. You are still breathing. Life challenged you, love bruised your heart, certain experiences left an ache in your soul, certain things along your journey made you question your capacity to heal or grow or twist your losses into lessons, and yet — you survived. Nothing, not even the heaviest moments, not even the situations that made you lose sight of your faith, had the ability to shatter you. And there is hope in that. There is strength in that.

If you feel like you cannot possibly heal from whatever it is that is weighing on your mind or your heart right now — remember all of the times you have found yourself here, and remember all of the ways in which you survived. Remember all of the ways you stretched into your growth, even when it was uncomfortable, and even when it didn't feel like it was happening. Remember how you, slowly but surely, caught your footing. Remember how you, slowly but surely, bandaged all that was hurting within you, and you learned how to be kinder to it, you learned how to heal it. You have fallen and you have risen time and time again. Do not doubt your capacity to do it again.

It is okay to want love.

At the end of the day, human beings need connection. We need one another. You can be the most foundationally sound person, you can be your own home, you can be so deeply content within your solitude — but that doesn't take away from the fact that love is a beautiful experience, that love is something worth searching for.

Love is something every single human being desires, and there are so many versions of love that you can find in this world. Love is seeing a smile crack across the fact of your best friend. Love is hearing your mother's voice. Love is pinned and blooming all around you, in the places that take your breath away, in the trips that change you, in the risks you take that force you to open up to the world and pour your curiosity into it.

But love is also seeing something astonishing and wanting to squeeze the hand of someone beside you, someone you have given your heart to. Love is hearing them singing in the shower and laughing at all of their horrible jokes, it's smiling to yourself and connecting with the fact that you found someone like you in a world of billions. Love is the hope you feel in your chest when you meet someone and you just know, in a bizarre and all-consuming way, that they are going to mean a lot to you, that you are going to clear a little corner of your soul out for them. Love is 2am grocery store runs for chocolate, and stolen moments on city streets, and curling into the whole of them on your way home after a long night. Love is the quietest kind of beauty. These moments seem small, but they aren't. They are so unbelievably full. And you can be whole on your own and still crave them. You can be whole on your own and still want to care deeply for another human being.

Embrace wanting to risk your heart. It is one of the greatest things you will ever do.

The truth is, we won't always end up with those we feel something deep and meaningful with. Some chapters of our lives are full and dizzying in the best way — with concrete endings and concrete closure. But some chapters end quickly, sometimes in the middle of the page, sometimes before we are even ready. We cannot control what comes to fruition in our lives. We cannot control how long someone chooses to love us; we cannot control how long someone chooses to stay. At the end of the day, all we can do is learn from the endings, all we can do is embrace the fact that for a moment in time, we felt something beautiful. For a moment in time, we felt something rare.

Stay open. Please, just stay open — because when you close yourself off to potential hurt, you also close yourself off to potential awe, potential joy. When you assume that you will never be seen and accepted for who you truly are, you rob yourself of the opportunity to be known, to be surprised by those who will show up in your life and hold your heart the way you have always hoped for it to be held. Yes, being vulnerable may hurt you. But it may heal you. There is always that risk — but you are here to risk your heart. So risk it, because there are situations and human beings in this world of billions that will meet you where you are, that will make you aware of just how beautiful it is to be fully open and seen and unafraid of falling. There are moments you're going to connect with, small and intense and deeply special moments, that will stick to your bones and remind you why you tried, why you took the chance. And it is up to you to tuck those moments into yourself for safekeeping, it is up to you to always believe in that beauty. Because this world will never be devoid of dark, but that just means there will also always be light.

One of the hardest lessons you will have to learn is that your life can be saturated with happiness, and you can still feel moments of deep emotion and sadness. You can be in a loving relationship, and you can still feel moments of intense loneliness. You can have access to the most beautiful human beings, and you can still feel like you're alone, like you are dealing with all that is going on within you on your own. You can do every single thing right — you can follow the advice of all of those who will tell you how to calm your mind, how to heal your hurt, you can affirm yourself each day, you can make self-care and the things you feel most passionate about the cornerstones of your whole world, and you can still feel like it is difficult to wake up in the morning.

Happiness within your life does not dismiss the fact that your brain works against you sometimes — that there are periods where it tries to taint the beauty your heart has felt. Happiness in your life does not dismiss the fact that anxiety sometimes makes you feel like you are hard to love, or like you have to apologize for the way you exist in this world. Happiness in your life does not dismiss the fact that your mind processes things differently, that it makes you feel things on a level that is often more severe than most would understand.

When a human being has a broken arm, we know how to fix it, we understand that we need to be gentle with it while it heals. But when it comes to our minds, sometimes we do not give ourselves that same level of grace, that same level of tenderness. Give yourself that tenderness. Give yourself permission to exist in whatever season you are in right now, give yourself permission to feel what you are feeling, instead of telling yourself that you aren't allowed to feel certain things due to the goodness that exists around you. Do whatever you have to do in order to heal. Do whatever you have to do in order to survive. Your journey is never going to be without the dark days — try your best to be compassionate with yourself when you cannot access your light.

This is your reminder — alone is not synonymous with not good enough. Alone is not a weakness, it is not something to be ashamed of. No, alone is a gift. It is a foundation, a steady ground within yourself that will be there whether or not you sleep beside the tired bones of another human being. Alone is knowledge, in yourself and in your hopes. Alone is a ruthless dedication to understanding your heart and fighting for what compels it after years of allowing for it to be loved in halves. Alone is not lonely. Alone is not broken. Alone is an anchoring, a healing — a reminder that the love you find within yourself will be yours forever, a reminder that you have the capacity to be your own home.

Choose happiness. Choose the kind of love that feels right, the kind of love that makes you understand why it didn't work out with anyone else. Choose the kind of life that makes you so damn happy you kept fighting for the things you wanted, for the way in which your heart asked you to believe in more. Choose yourself, unapologetically and without guilt — the way you choose others. Show up for yourself. Give yourself permission to hope, to care, to trust in the things you deeply crave from life. Choose letting go. Choose forgiveness, choose to turn your losses into lessons. Choose to move forward, into the kind of story that fulfills you, into the kind of person that holds your heart just as carefully as you hold theirs, into the kind of happiness that exists because you chose to fight for it, and never stop fighting for it. Never stop.

Some days you are going to wake up and things will feel calm. Your vision will be clear, the world will be yours. You will dance upon the ashes of your past and your body will ache with an overwhelming feeling of joy. Other days, you will have a hard time twisting your scars into lessons. Your bed will seem like the safest place on this whole entire planet.

There are going to be days where your bones feel heavy under the weight of all the love you hold within yourself, and this will be a good thing. You will be thankful for your ability to feel, for your ability to give to another human being a love that is flourishing and alive underneath your skin. Then will come the days where you feel like you have nothing left within you to give, the days that remind you of how much you had before you lost it all, how your affection was never properly reciprocated. You will wonder if you love too deeply; you will wonder if you care too openly.

On either of these days it is important to remember that you cannot control the randomness of life or any of its fickle flashes. Some mornings you will wake up to a sapphire sky and you will breathe, you will cry. On others you will rejoice, you will laugh with all of the vigor in your body. There are going to be moments in life that propel you forward, and there will be those that grab you by the ankles and drag you three steps in the opposite direction. Love will build you the most exquisite house made of paper and glass just to blow it down; it will grow you and it will tear you apart in the process. On most days it won't make sense, and that is the point — life is a mess. Everything about it is a giant hurricane that we will never truly comprehend, that we will never be able to contain, but that is what makes it so stunning, that is what makes it perfect.

As William Lear famously said, "It's all a mess – the hair, the bed, the words, the heart. Life." It is all a mess, but we cannot deny the fact that it is magic. We cannot deny the fact that it is frustrating and stunning, empty and full at the exact same time, overflowing with opportunities to feel and grow and swallow the sun whole if we truly wanted to. We must remind ourselves that life is never going to slow down, it is never going to simplify, and we must come to terms with that — for if we search for routine, the ordinary will kill us before the sadness does.

Embrace the entropy in life. You were bred from storms; that is why you are primarily water. You were created from white-hot heat and from atoms that will never stop vibrating and shaking within you, so do not vilify your heart when it quakes, do not condemn your life when it surges and when it falls. Embrace its pulse and the randomness of it all; embrace its disorder.

Life is a mess — yes, but my god, is it ever a beautiful one.

When you are trying to let go of someone who cannot hold your heart, when you are trying to move on from someone who cannot care for you the way you deserve to be cared for, when you are trying to gather the courage to walk away from the person who only ever makes you feel like you are hard to love — remember what you are worthy of.

Because don't you deserve to find someone who chooses you the way you choose them? Don't you deserve to find someone who reciprocates your love, who wants to hold you on the days that feel dark and devoid of light, who wants to encourage your growth and see you realize your dreams and celebrate birthdays with you, and milestones with you, and make the sunniest kind of memories with you?

Don't you deserve to find someone who wants to stand by your side, firmly, and know deeply in their heart that you are something special, that you are their favorite thing? Don't you deserve to find someone who sees you — who actually sees you, in all that is light and all that is dark within you, in all of your mess and all of your virtue? Don't you deserve someone who loves you there?

Don't you deserve to find someone who knows, with a ruthless certainty, that they found the kind of human being they want to protect? The kind of human being they want to nurture, and encourage, and experience the smallest most nameless things with? Don't you deserve that kind of beauty? That kind of peace?

Don't you deserve to find someone who shows up? Someone who wants to laugh with you in bed at 2am when you both can't sleep? Someone who wants to wrap you up between their arms on a rainy day? Someone who wants to be the reason a smile dances across your face? Someone who wants to make dinner with you, and slow-dance in the kitchen with you, and squeeze your hand at the scary parts of the movie you're watching together? Don't you deserve someone who wants all of that? Someone who wants to be in your life? Someone who chooses depth over distance?

Let go of anything that does not serve that version of love. Let go of anything that does not hold your heart. Let go of those who love you in halves, who will never be able to give you what you deeply desire. Do not hold space in your heart for those who are not showing up to claim it. You deserve good love. Release anything that does not honor that.

Please, whatever you do — just leap towards tenderness. Leap towards connection. We are all afraid to say too much, to feel too deeply, to let people know what they mean to us. But caring is not synonymous with crazy. Expressing to someone how special they are to you will make you vulnerable. There is no denying that. However, that is nothing to be ashamed of. There is something breathtakingly beautiful in the moments of smaller magic that occur when you strip down and are honest with those who are important to you, when you choose to slam your heart into those who ignite something within it, when you express. So, express. Express, express, express. Open yourself up, do not harden yourself to the world, and be bold in who, and how, you love. There is courage in that.

Connections cannot be measured in time, but rather in how deeply they help you to see yourself. See, you can love someone for years and lose yourself. And yet, you can know someone for a week and see your whole soul in another human being. There are no rules when it comes to the heart and where it feels most safe. There are no timelines for this kind of depth. You just have to trust it. You just have to see it for what it is and understand that the universe sometimes fights for souls to find one another. It is not to be questioned. It is not to be compared. It is simply just meant to be felt. Have the courage to feel it.

Don't vilify your heart for holding onto the memory of someone who made it feel deeply. Don't bankrupt yourself of that nostalgia. Find grace within the fact that you may always hold pieces of them inside of you.

When you connect with someone, not just on a surface level, but in a way that makes you want to make them a home within yourself — that stays with you. See, we all have different rooms within our hearts dedicated to those we once loved. Those rooms are filled with the echoes of our past. Those rooms are filled with all of the inside jokes, all of those firsts, all of those feelings that made your stomach flip and your chest tighten with excitement. Those rooms are stacked full with the layers of those we once embraced — they are filled with their fears and their virtues and all of the things they confided in you, all of the moments you truly saw them lift their veil and show you who they were behind their masks. And while it is okay to close the door to those rooms, while it is okay to move forward, that does not mean they don't exist. That does not mean they suddenly fail to take up space within your heart.

Because the truth is — they will always take up space. You don't just forget the people who made you believe in something rare. You don't forget the people who made you feel something special.

When you can stand on your own solid foundation, as your own person, as someone who is growing on your own terms and healing on your own terms and not looking at love as a means of completion, but rather, complementation — that is where the most beautiful kind of connections are grown, that is where the most inspiring kind of hope is discovered. Love transforms. You aren't asking for someone to deplete parts of their world in order to fit within yours, and vice versa. You're finding harmony within those worlds. You coexist.

Trust me when I say that the strongest love you will ever experience will exist within ultimate freedom. The freedom to be your own individual self, the freedom to chase what ignites you, the freedom to figure out what kind of person you want to be and the freedom to do everything you can in order to meet that potential. When you understand that love is union, that you do not have to lose yourself within it, you can encourage its growth without thinking that that growth will take away from the relationship or crack the foundation. You aren't afraid of someone chasing their dreams, or changing, or evolving into themselves, because you are doing the same. You are doing it side by side.

When it comes to your heart, do not rush your healing. In a society that is so deeply fixated on instant gratification, just be the person who accepts that moving on will not happen overnight. Do not try to dismiss your feelings or sweep them under the rug. Take your time. Be gentle with yourself.

Because the truth is, if you cared about someone, if you let them leave pieces of themselves littered within your memories, knotted to your heart, you are going to have to come to terms with the fact that you will not move on in an instant. You will slowly let go, in so many different ways, in so many different phases. Your healing will find you in places you never thought it would. You will let go in the obvious, tangible ways — in removing their things from your apartment, in taking down the photos from your wall, in learning how to sleep in the middle of the bed again, in learning how to make just one cup of coffee in the morning.

But there are also moments in life, unexpected and jarring, that will come out of nowhere and those will be healing moments, too. You will let go of them when you smell their perfume in public and it doesn't make your stomach flip. You will let go of them when your song comes on the radio and it doesn't scratch painfully at the memory of what it felt like to fall in love with them. You will let go of them when you hear that they were out with another person, that they are slowly opening their heart to the world again. You will let go when you decide to do the same. And this doesn't mean that you are fully healed, but this means that you are taking the steps towards your hearts rebuilding. That you are learning how to exist with the memory of them, that you are not trying to rush it out the door, but rather, you are learning how to be thankful for it, how to slowly appreciate it for what it has taught you without needing it back.

Be patient with your healing. It is happening, even when you cannot feel it.

I need you to understand that it is okay to have a soul that is both tender and tired. I need you to understand that it is okay to be gentle with yourself, that is okay to feel what you are feeling, that it is okay to let it all crack within the weight of your bones. I need you to know that it is okay to not be okay, that it is okay to feel sad even if you do not fully understand it. I need you to know that you do not have to live in one extreme. That you do not have to force yourself to feel perpetual happiness, that you do not have to sit with your damage and make a home out of it. I need you to know that you exist in multitudes. I need you to know that you are the product of what is both hopeful and haunted within you, and it is okay to exist in this world as someone who is simply figuring out how to balance that.

Because this is what they don't tell you — being a human is both beautiful and burdensome. It is a confusing and messy thing. Life will amaze you in the most stunning ways, and it will also break your heart. Life will gift you the kinds of lessons that grow you and build you and help for you to bloom into the person you have always hoped to be, but it will also carry within it the kinds of losses that stay with you, that change you and mold you in uncomfortable ways. Life will demand for you to do the work, for you to understand yourself, for you to heal even when it hurts. For you to be brave, for you to fight for yourself.

At the end of the day, bravery isn't a battlefield. It isn't fast cars or stunted risk. Bravery is the quietest thing you will ever know. Bravery is getting up in the morning when your bones are heavy and your heart does not want the light to crack within it. Bravery is leaning into what aches, it is looking it in the face, giving it a name and confronting it for what it is. Bravery is being gentle with yourself, especially when it isn't convenient or easy, especially when you are not a shining example of the person you strive to be. Bravery is forgiving yourself, it is the work you do within your soul that is dirty and difficult and demanding.

But most of all, bravery is the way you stretch towards the light. It is the way you bloom in the direction of goodness, even when you may not know what you are reaching for. Bravery is allowing yourself to believe that you are growing, even when it does not feel like it. Bravery is trusting yourself even when you do not recognize the path. Bravery is knowing that there is more for you, that you will have the ability to save yourself like you always have before; that you will survive.

Above all else, I hope you give yourself permission to believe that you are not defined by a person's inability to love you or by a person's inability to choose you. I hope you do not abandon who you are even though they did. I hope you do not neglect or question yourself even though they did. I hope you remember to love yourself better than they could, I hope you learn how to give yourself that kind of strength. I hope you remind yourself that you are rare, that you hold value here. I hope seasons of being misunderstood, of being unappreciated, do not cause you to see yourself through the eyes of those who could not celebrate you or support you. Above all else, I hope you connect with just how worthy you have always been. I hope you give yourself permission to be all that you are.

You can still care
for the people who hurt you,
but that does not change the fact
that you have to let them go.

This is your reminder — sometimes your biggest losses end up introducing you to your biggest gains.

Sometimes, you do not end up with the person your heart chooses. Sometimes, you cannot make your love a one-size-fits-all for the circumstances, or the opportunities, or the changes that are unfolding in your life. Sometimes you have to lay all of your hope down; you have to stop it from pouring out of you and into a love that will never be nourished enough to meet you where you are right now. But you cannot forget that in walking away, in creating that space, you are giving yourself the opportunity to meet the person who will stay. The person who shows up for you. The person who will understand the depth of your feeling, the person who will make you understand why it never worked out with anyone else, and you are going to be so glad that you worked through the loss, that you let go with grace, because it led you to them.

Sometimes, the hardest seasons of your life are growing you into a version of yourself that recognizes your own strength, that believes in your capacity to rebuild even the most broken parts of who you are. Sometimes, it is within those moments, it is within that dark, where you meet your survival, where you learn to weather whatever storm life manages to send your way. And sometimes, you will not know where this quiet power has come from, you will not know how or when the healing began, but it will be there. It will always arrive, quietly in the night, after weeks, or months, or years of pushing your way into the world. And it is within that reality, it is within that softening, that you will be reminded of all the ways you continue to beat the odds. It is within that journey, it is within that fight, where you will be reminded of how you overcame all of the things you once thought would defeat you.

At the end of the day, you must remember this — energy cannot be created or destroyed, it can only be transformed. The universe does not take without giving, and it is within the messiness, and the aches of life, where you will finally be introduced to the beauty, where you will finally be introduced to the light.

Moving on is not about forgetting, is not about denying the memory. Moving on is about having gratitude for what has impacted your heart without having to dismiss your experience or disregard it. Moving on is about folding the memory into yourself — letting it remind you that you fought for something, that you tried, that you felt.

You deserve to be loved
and chosen —

not almost loved,
or almost chosen.

The truth is — no one comes out of life unscathed. No one navigates their journey without experiencing certain things that leave a mark, without experiencing certain things that weigh heavily within their souls. The truth is – we have all been hurt at the hands of others. We have all been weathered by things we may not have always deserved, by jarring and unexpected circumstances. We all hold nostalgia within us, the kind that has scarred our souls, the kind that swirls together hurt and hope within a human being. We are all just learning how to find understanding within those aches, we are all just learning how to seek forgiveness, how to believe in what the storms were teaching us. The truth is — we are all just trying to heal from the things we don't often talk about; we are all just trying to heal from the things we don't quite understand.

And the truth is, because of that, because we have been wounded, because we walk around with so much of our past within ourselves, because we allow for it to tell us who we are and what we are worthy of, because we allow for it to convince us of our value — we have all been the person who makes the mistake. We have all been the kind of human being who could not show up. We have all been the kind of person who could not love someone beautifully, who could not connect at the time. We have all been the kind of person who fumbles with the weight of evolution, with the weight of wanting to be better, with the weight of knowing that there is a kinder version of ourselves out there, a version that has done the work, that has reconciled the ways in which the world wasn't always kind to it. We have all been hurt in ways we may not be able to express, in ways we may not have healed, in ways that stick.

We are all just hoping that the world has compassion for us within that hurt. Within that experience. We are all hoping that the world will see the ways in which we have tried to forgive ourselves for the human beings we used to be. We are all hoping that those we love will recognize our fight, will see the ways in which we have tried to learn from the losses, the ways in which we have tried to be kinder to our wounds so they do not wound others. We are all just hoping to find the kind of human beings who understand, human beings who know what it is like to hold all of that within themselves.

Please, whatever you do — just be the kind of human being who believes in others. Normalize second chances. Normalize having compassion for someone who needed to walk away in order to grow and heal. Normalize believing human beings who express that they have done the work, who have proven that they are ready and willing to show up and care for you the way you deserve to be cared for. Normalize empathy. Normalize tenderness. Normalize understanding that some people have so many worlds within themselves, memories tucked into their minds, that they are trying to nurture, that they are trying to heal. We are all becoming. We are all growing in the dark, we are all carrying the weight of certain things we did not ask to hold. We are all learning how to set that weight down. How to be lighter. Always remind yourself of that. Always try your best to keep love in the equation.

Who would you be if you set what hurts down? Who would you be without the relationships in your life that do not serve you, without the things in your life that do not reach for you with the same depth and the same hopefulness you reach for them? Who would you be without the opinions of the outside world, without the expectations; who would you be if you knew that your soul would not be judged, that the version of yourself you presented to the world was the purest reflection of who you were inside? Who would you be if you let go? If you did not try to control, if you let things flow through your life like rain? Who would you be if you gave yourself permission to change, if you gave yourself permission to do things differently? Who would you be if you went ruthlessly in the direction of what you truly desired in life, if you committed yourself to existing in a way that made you happy on your own terms? Who would you be if you finally decided, outside of outward validation, outside of external success, that you were worthy? That you were valued? That you did not have to be perfect in order to be loved? Who would you be?

Always choose to care. Choose to stay messy-hearted in a world that may not always be kind to you. Choose to do whatever you have to do to make it to tomorrow; choose to get up in the morning when you do not want to, choose to face what is scarred within you — please, just work every single day to be gentle and soft with yourself, even when you have been given every reason to harden. Choose to believe in something hopeful; choose to feel everything intensely, and do not apologize for your power, your hope, or the way you slam yourself into the human beings you meet. Choose to shout your love from rooftops, choose to share your heart with the world. Choose to fight — to be better, to heal even when it hurts, to believe with everything you hold within yourself that you have purpose here and that you belong here — that you deserve to take up space.

At the end of the day, it is quite simple — there are so many uncertain and confusing things in life, but love should never be one of them. Love should never be one of them.

If you have lost someone that was once a beautiful part of your life, remind yourself that energy cannot be created or destroyed, it can only be transformed — that is a scientific law. Everything in this world exists within a cycle — our bodies, the nature around us, the stars, the whole entire universe. Everything is constantly going through phases of life and death, and if we think of that law, we can appreciate those periods of evolution, those periods of death, and reframe that as periods of transformation. The energy that exists within that person, the love you shared, the hope you felt — it is never gone. It exists out in the world somewhere.

When you are mourning the loss of a human being, when the grief feels heavy and you wish that they could be experiencing certain things beside you, that you could just share one more moment with them, that you could make just one more memory — remind yourself of that law. They may not be in your life in the way you remember them, but their energy, and their love, and their heart, still exists in this world. They are all around you. They are always with you.

Because the truth is — we never really lose the people we lose. They are in the sunsets, and in the rain, and in the forests, and in laughter, and music that takes our breath away. We never really lose their love, their beauty, because that energy doesn't disappear — it finds new ways to reach you. Pay attention.

Not everyone you are
ready to love will be ready
to be loved by you.

The hardest thing you will have to do in life is to let go of the people you may want to hold onto. Sometimes, you will have to settle for loving someone from a distance, and that is okay. Because if you cannot show up for another human being the way you know you should, if someone cannot love you the way you need to be loved right now, if circumstance or space or the messiness of life is getting in the way of giving your whole self and nothing less than that to another human being, then you have to be honest. Do not suffocate your love. Do not ignore the way someone makes you feel about yourself in order to keep them in your life, do not ask for something to be more than it can be right now. Instead, appreciate it for what it was, appreciate the lessons it grew within you, appreciate the beauty you were able to feel, and appreciate the fact that in those ways, in those memories, it will be yours forever.

You did not lose; you got lucky. You got lucky enough to meet someone who showed you that the world still had goodness inside of it. That there were souls within this universe that felt as deeply, and cared as feverishly, and went to war for others as delicately as you did. You got lucky because you were shown, with a gravity you still may not understand, that you were seen, that you were mirrored in other people, that your soul was not alone, that your heart was not a patchwork of memories that would never fit together again.

You did not lose; you got lucky. You got lucky enough to spend time with someone who wanted to experience the world through your eyes. Who wanted to watch old movies and listen to rainstorms with you and feel your eyelashes blink across their neck. You got lucky enough to have slow conversations with a human being who ignited your every cell, who made you want to be better, who sat you down and stretched you out and made you uncomfortable enough to expand. You got lucky. Lucky enough to meet someone who understood your silent languages, the small and nameless ways you said I love you by pulling them closer in bed or making sure that they got home safely or squeezing their thigh when you heard their voice crack on a goodbye.

You did not lose; you got lucky. You got lucky because you met someone who, for a moment in time, was able to squeeze all of your broken pieces back together. You met someone who did not judge you for the ways in which you had to kill your sadness, for the things you chased or sought out or broke in your past looking to understand yourself a little more, looking to salve the wounds, looking to fill the voids. You got lucky. Lucky enough to meet someone who plucked anxiety out of your chest like splinters, who poured calm into the parts of you that no one else clapped for. You got lucky enough to meet someone who was not threatened by who you were, by who you had to be to save yourself, because they knew it led you to them.

No, you did not lose — you got lucky. You got lucky because time did not choose to separate you, time did not choose to keep you two apart, did not choose to send you to a different coffee shop or party or moment that would have gifted you a different brush with a different fate. You got lucky. Lucky enough to exist at the same time, lucky enough to have found them, to have experienced them, to have been given the opportunity to love them the way you loved them. You got lucky because the universe fought for your souls to be together, it fought to show you that within a stranger there was a safe place, there was, even if temporary, even if for a moment frozen in time, the existence of hope within another human being.

And even if you were not loved like this, you are still lucky. See, sometimes people come into our lives and they love us like sunrises — filling our hearts with the melted hues of tenderness and peace, their energy clouding our bones with the breathtaking pinks and the purples of feeling, only ever leaving us softer, and kinder to ourselves, only ever taking our breath away.

But sometimes, sometimes people come into our lives and they love us like hurricanes — filling our hearts with tempered squalls of doubt and dishonesty, their actions clouding our minds with the blackened blues and grays of questioning our hearts, of questioning our worth, or questioning if we love too hard, if we feel too deeply, if we are simply too much to hold. The hardest lesson you will ever have to learn is that this too is a gift. To have been loved in halves, to have been loved by someone who could not understand what it meant to hold such a rare and hopeful thing, is to have been loved by someone who taught you how to walk away. How to choose yourself for once, how to stand up for your worth and for the way you exist in this world. At the end of the day, they may not have loved you, but they did teach you how to survive the wreckage, how to endure the storm, and how to rebuild.

They may not have loved you, but you still risked your heart. You still tried for something. You still believed. And that is what makes you lucky, because that is what has made you strong.

Bad timing doesn't exist. The people your heart chooses at what it thinks is the wrong time are simply just the wrong people. They are simply just the ones who were meant to get away. They were simply just the ones who were never meant to stay. Because at the end of the day, the right people fight for you. The right people show up. The right people care, not only when life is convenient, but when it is difficult and messy and it aches all over. The right people take the chance; they choose you just as confidently as you choose them. They hand you their heart. They bet on you. They believe in what you share with a ruthless conviction, with a hope that spills out of them. Have the courage to wait for these people. Do not settle for half-loves, do not settle for someone who does not see the value in holding your heart. The people who walk away from you because the timing is not right are simply just the people who are not willing to put the right amount of time into you. Let that be your closure.

Sometimes, you have to choose yourself. Sometimes, you have to choose your healing, no matter how hard you want to keep fighting, no matter how deeply you care. See, when your heart chooses someone who does not choose it back, when your tender soul fights for someone who will not fight for it, when you make the effort to show up for someone who does not care, or make the effort, to show up for you — you must walk away. You must give yourself the closure you so desperately seek. You must give yourself permission to move forward, to let go, to believe in the fact that you deserve to be loved by someone who will look at you and know that you are enough. Because if there is one thing life has taught me, it is that love, genuine love, should never make you feel like you are too much, it should never make you feel like a difficult person to care for. If there is one thing life has taught me, it is that love, worthwhile love, should never make you quiet your heartbeat, it should never be something you have to beg for. So please, if you still find yourself chasing after someone who is not chasing after you — stop running towards those dead ends and instead start running toward yourself.

I am sorry that the world wasn't always kind to you.

I am sorry that the world wasn't always kind to your heart. I am sorry that you placed your tenderness into the hands of those who fumbled with the weight of it, that you believed in people who made you feel like you were difficult to love, that you gave so much of your hope to people who made you feel like you had to apologize for the way you cared. I am sorry that you experienced certain things at the hands of love that caused you to stop believing its kindness, that made you question if you were worthy of experiencing something real, and honest, and dedicated. I am sorry that you loved human beings who did not love themselves. I am sorry that you loved human beings who did not try to take care of you. I am sorry that you lost sight of your softness for a moment in time. I am sorry that love wasn't always your safe place, wasn't always compassionate towards you.

I am sorry that the world sometimes failed to protect your soul. That the universe sent you certain human beings who were hurt, and in turn, they hurt you. I am sorry that you had to carry all of that weight inside of yourself. I am sorry for the things you had to endure, for the ways in which the world cracked pain into your life, for the ways in which it met you with things you were not prepared for, circumstances you could not weather on your own.

I am sorry that the world took so much from you. That it made you experience things you were too young to experience. That it took away your mother, your father. I am sorry that the world took away your courage, that there were mornings you felt like the heaviness of merely existing was too much of a load to carry. I am sorry that the world took so many pieces of you, that it walked away with so much of your hope when you needed it the most, when you were just looking for a soft place to land. I am sorry that you were not held there. I am sorry that you had to do it alone.

I am sorry that the world wasn't always kind to you. I am sorry that you had to learn certain things in ways that will stay with you forever. I am sorry. I am sorry.

But I am proud of you for being here. I am proud of you for trying to heal in the midst of all that felt unfair and cruel. I am proud of you for fighting to stay here. I am proud of you for the person you were, for the person you became, for the way you dug yourself out of the dark, for the way you pushed through the shadow. I am proud of you for your hope. I am proud of you for your belief in the goodness, for the way you focused on it when so many aspects of your life tried to convince you that it did not exist. I am proud of you for choosing to survive. I am proud of you. You did not deserve what happened to you. You did not deserve what you experienced. But here you are. Here you are.

At the end of the day, I just want to be proud of the person I have become.

At the end of the day, I want to be proud of the way I loved, I want to be proud of the way I placed my heart into the hands of others. I want to be proud of the way I chose vulnerability, of the way I chose tenderness; how I never stopped choosing it no matter what my soul experienced at the hands of being the kind of human being who loved deeply in this world. At the end of the day, I want to be proud of the way I fought for others, of the way I dedicated myself to making them feel seen and understood; I want to be proud of the way I showed up, of the way I tried my best to speak beauty into the parts of them that no one else clapped for. At the end of the day, I want to be proud of the way I did not let fear convince me to keep myself hidden from others; I want to be proud of the way I cared.

At the end of the day, I want to be proud of the way I fought to be here. At the end of the day, I want to be proud of the way I taught myself a version of strength that was different than the one the world had tried so hard to instill within me. I want to be proud of the way I reframed bravery, of how I made it into something that was soft. At the end of the day, I want to be proud of the way I worked through my dark, I want to be proud of the way I sat down with what was heavy and unresolved within me, I want to be proud of the way I healed even when it hurt. At the end of the day, I want to be proud of the way I tucked hope into myself for safekeeping, I want to be proud of the way I believed that there was more to experience at the hands of life, that the beauty I had yet to feel existed in this world. At the end of the day, I want to be proud of the way I survived.

At the end of the day, I want to be proud of the way I showed up. Of the way I existed in this world, of the way I dedicated myself to living the kind of life that was full, that allowed for happiness, and sadness, and growth to flow through me like rain. At the end of the day, I want to be proud of the way I fell in love with my life, of the way I fell in love with a version of happiness that I created from the deepest parts of my soul. At the end of the day, I want to be proud of the fact that I never took a back seat to my pain, that I never let my past convince me that I did not deserve the potential the future was holding for me. I want to be proud of the way I moved in the direction of life, in the direction of living, in the direction of experience, in the direction of love. At the end of the day, I want to be proud of the way I risked my soul, I want to be proud of the way I honored it.

Because, at the end of the day — I want to leave this world with a heart that is worn-out and tender all over, a heart that aches from loving, and feeling, and caring in the best way possible. I want to leave this world knowing that I poured love into everything I did, that I crashed my soul into each and every single day, that I tried for something while I was here. At the end of the day, I just want to be proud of the person I have become. I just want to be proud of the way I connected.

*

BIANCA SPARACINO is a writer from Toronto. She wrote this for you.

instagram.com/rainbowsalt
facebook.com/rainbowsalt

thoughtcatalog.com/bianca-sparacino

Other THOUGHT CATALOG titles
published by AMARYLLIS in India

THE PIVOT YEAR

101 ESSAYS THAT WILL CHANGE
THE WAY YOU THINK

THE MOUNTAIN IS YOU

WHEN YOU'RE READY THIS IS HOW YOU HEAL

CEREMONY

THIS WAS MEANT TO FIND YOU:
WHEN YOU NEEDED IT MOST

THIS IS ME LETTING YOU GO

SALT WATER

EVERYTHING YOU'LL EVER NEED
YOU CAN FIND WITHIN YOURSELF

THE HUMAN ELEMENT

THE STRENGTH IN OUR SCARS

THE TRUTH ABOUT EVERYTHING

ALL THE WORDS I SHOULD HAVE SAID

BEAUTY IN THE STILLNESS

YOU'RE OVERTHINKING IT